HACKING With SMART PHONES

Disclaimer

This book is designed to provide a brief insight on the elementary maneuvers of a hacker and how can one make themselves digitally secure. This book is a very basic guide on hacking. The author and publisher are not offering it as legal, accounting, or other professional services advice.

Preface

At a recent event I came across someone who had read both my previous books but was still unable to grasp anything about hacking. The language and tasks discussed in my former books are very complex. He asked me to write something basic that everyone can understand.

So, I thought to write about Hacking with a Smartphones, a readily available tool to everyone in this 21st Century. Even a rickshaw driver today who earns hundred rupees a day owns a Smartphone.

Understandably, none of us want our data to be hacked by a rickshaw driver, but the tricks and methods in this book have been explained so easily that even they can clench it.

With the craze of e-shopping and net banking increasing the rate of cyber crime is increasing too. This book will tell you simple countermeasures about smart phones and digital security, they are simple but dangerous.

Note: Don't expect big hacking techniques through this book, it may disappoint you.

Author

Trishneet Arora is an Indian author, cyber security expert, and entrepreneur. Arora has written books on various topics related to Cyber Security, Ethical Hacking and Web Defense.

With no family background in computers, Arora is a first-generation entrepreneur. He set up his own company - TAC Security Solutions, which is into providing security to the corporate companies against any data theft and network vulnerabilities. Some of TAC's prominent corporate clients include: Reliance Industries, Amul, CBI, Avon Cycles, Punjab and Gujrat Police.

He also helps Punjab and Gujrat police in training senior level officers and cracking down cyber crime.

On the 65th Republic Day Chief Minister of Punjab, **Parkash Singh Badal** bestowed a *'State Award'* upon Arora. He also received the *Punjab Icon Award 2015* in Mumbai by PCHB.

Content

1. Android vs iOS

2. How to Spy on Android Phone?

3. How to remotely access your mobile phone?

4. How to retrieve deleted Whatsapp messages (android)?

5. What is the use of HTTPS?

6. Your Location Has Been Shared, You don't know right?

7. How to find a lost iPhone?

8. How to unlock an iPhone passcode?

9. How to get fake likes on an *Instagram* post?

10. How to get fake followers on *Instagram*?

1. Android vs iOS

Most of the applications in our Smartphone like Snapchat, Flipkart, Shazam etc are manually downloaded by us.

Prior to their installation such apps always demand certain kind of permissions:

- Access to Messages
- GPS Location
- Contacts
- Call details
- Photos
- Videos
- And many more

We users are left with no option other than to grant them the permission to access our personal data and hope that these gigantic companies will not exploit it.

App info

Permissions

This app can access the following on your phone:

- read phone status and identity
- receive text messages (SMS)
- send SMS messages
  - this may cost you money
- take pictures and videos
- record audio
- approximate location (network-based)
- precise location (GPS and network-based)
- modify your contacts
- read your contacts

So the question that arises here is that can we secure our mobile devices at all?

Yes - Use **NOKIA 1100**. - Still you may not be 100% secure.

Better idea! - **"Stop using gadgets totally"**

Usage of mobile phones and digital gadgets has never been safe.

We just need to retain this in our minds that we are HACKED! Advisably hence avoid putting any confidential data in your mobile phones.

Finally lets talk about the chapter's title - Which operating system is more secure?

Personally, I consider IOS a much more safer platform than Android. Android users have various stores from which they can download apps. Hence the chances of an unsourced application getting installed and remotely accessing our mobile phones is high.

iOS users on the other hand can only download apps from App Store, where all the applications are fully vetted before being made available. Hackers and security researchers have been trying hard to sell malware as an application in the App Store but are repeatedly ineffective in front of the resilient and strong Apple Inc. Security. App Store provides users with the certainty that the apps they download have been pretested by Apple.

However, you can't say IOS is 100% invincible. For instance take the incident of Charlie Miller, a security researcher who deliberately created a suspicious application and submitted it to Apple. Initially Apple approved the application; as a result the app unearthed a bug in the iOS. Though Apple soon smelt the rat and suspended Charlie's developer account for one year.

2. How to SPY on an Android Phone?

I was invited as a speaker at the Cyber Threats Summit Delhi 2014. The summit agenda was Corporate IT Security, so it was understood that my talkshould be on Network Security, Data Security and Online Financial Frauds. In my five hour journey from Chandigarh to New Delhi I prepared my presentation on the same. I reached the venue an hour prior to my speech and started mingling with my friends and co workers at the event.

Other speakers in my panel were Mr. AnirbanSen Gupta, Director-Cyber Frauds at PwC India, Mr. RajenderaKhetal, President-ISACA Delhi, and Mr. J.S Salonki from Mahindra Special Services Group. Though every orator spoke very well, the audience seemed disappointed and unhappy. Experts in their field, the speakers spoke about their market incidents and case studies of network and data security. The speeches were more theoretical than practical.

It was clear to me that if I were to present what I had prepared, the audience would kill me. With just 40 minutes remaining to my speech I decided to turn the whole presentation to *Mobile Hacking*.

Before I started speaking Mr.Gupta addressed the conference with a lot enlightening details and it was good but the audience was still longing for practical demonstration.

After announcing my name the Anchor started staring at me, a teenage boy. She was wondering what I was doing in the midst of such big corporate giants.

I started, "Though the audience has becomefar less than I saw before lunch, whoever is here their presence matter to me a lot. Since the morning you are listening about Data Security, Network Security, and Hacking! But nobody is telling you how it happens. Speakers are talking about Rocket Science Hacking, Nuclear Hacking butthe point is HOW….."

I asked the audience for a cellphone. But no one volunteered, they were scared, finally Mr.Gupta handed over to me his sexy HTC phone. I fiddled around withit for some seconds and asked Mr.Gupta that since he was talking about mail hacking and confidential data, would he like to see his data in my cloud house. I can't describe or tell you the expression of the audience when I demonstrated the same.

But you can definitely see the demonstration…

I just had to download a spy app on his phone and the access was with me.

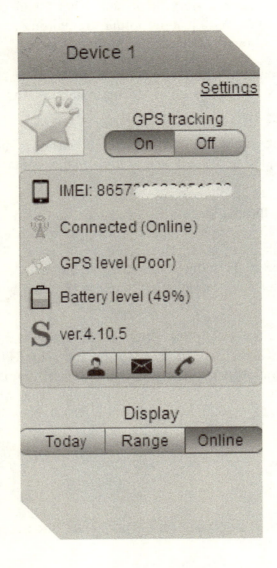

Create an id at *spy2mobile.com*

Go to the victim's mobile browser and open URL:

www.spy2mobile.com/d

After the installation it will ask for your email address. (Mention the same email address that you registered at *spy2mobile.com*.

Here you go.

You can get entree to everything of the victim.

Call logs, Messages, Location and Whats App chat too. Most interesting part is that it all happens in just 2-3 minutes.

The victim will not be able to see any application in the main menu until he/she doesn't analyze the application manager.

3. How to remotely access your mobile phone?

Few years back I was in Gujarat for some work. The client's office was roughly 60 km far from my hotel. Our meeting was fixed for 10am in the morning and like every other Indian I was late. I started from my hotel at 9:46 am itself and started working on my laptop on the way. F**k! Halfway through I realized that I had left my tab back in the room. All my contacts and data were saved on it and my tab was not connected to cloud. I was upset and angry. I realized that this could have happened to anyone.

In the search for a solution to this often made human error, I found a very interesting application called *"Airdroid"*

Airdroid helps you to access your android phone or tablet distantly. I went back at my room in the evening and installed that application.

Here is the

demonstration…..

1. Create an account in *Airdroid.com*

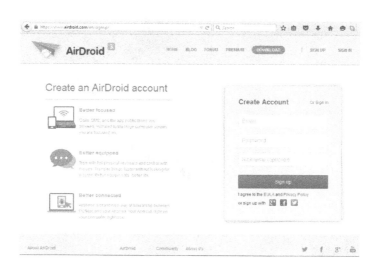

2. Install AirDroid on your Android phone.
3. Login at *web.AirDroid.com* on your laptop browser.
4. Login to AirDroid App on your mobile phone with same user name and password.
5. Go to web.Airdroid.com on your laptop browser and check if your device is connected.

Now it doesn't matter where your android device is. You can access anything and everything with the help of Airdroid and a good internet connection; Messages, Apps, Videos, Camera, Files, Call Logs, Photos and Contacts too.

4. How to retrieve deleted Whatsapp messages? (Android)

I came across a case of match fixing where the convicts communicated over Whatsapp. The match fixer and the player used Whatsapp to fix their deal in the belief that deleted what's app conversation is impossible to recover. Repeatedly they made their plans and then deleted their Whastapp chat.

Authorities slowly developed a suspicion over them but were unsuccessful in finding any substantial evidence. The investigation became tough and staggered.

But they were not aware, *"Nothing is impossible for HACKERS"*

Just few steps and you can recover all chats.

1. Go to File Manager in the Mobile

2. Follow the white colored folder at the border
3. The chat files here are in the encrypted form.

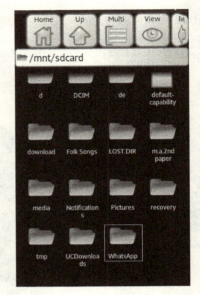

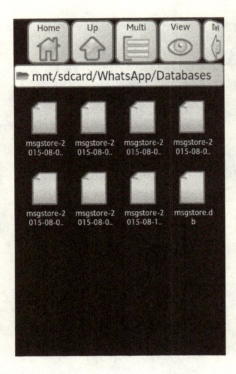

4. Open Recovermessages.com on your laptop or computer browser and decrypt the encrypted files and see the chats.

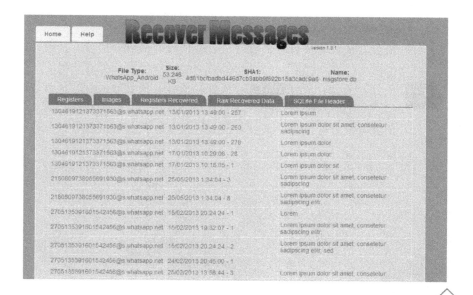

5. What is use of HTTP*S*?

Incorrectly most of people think that *"S"* stands for Secure..

Once while performing Penetration Testing and Vulnerability Assessment for a client in Dubai, I started playing with their network. I endeavored the Man-in-Middle attack. Yeah, I was *Middle* in their network. Users in their network accessed many servers, web pages and they logged in into that and which sites were *HTTP only* they saved passwords and username detail for Man(me) who was Middle in their network and HTTPS didn't saved it for me ☹ ….. You can see the *Snapshots* below.

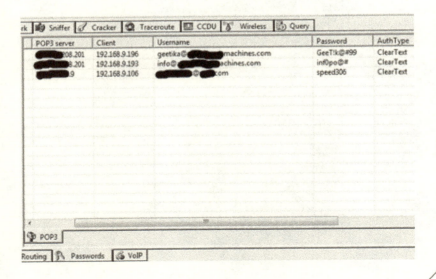

6. Your Location has been shared, you don't know right?

Every Android user use free or paid apps. As discussed in the earlier chapters most of these people are unaware of how many times these applications have shared their sensitive information with third parties

So one should know if their location is being spyied or not.

Let me tell you an interesting tale, I was sitting with the Managing Director of one of the India's top most company in Mumbai. He confidently told me "I am secure, I am using an antivirus in mobile phone." I just politely asked him, "If you don't mind Mr. Singh, may I analyze your secure phone?" After few seconds, Mr. Singh was in sheer astonishment.

He said: "Are you kidding me? Just coz of these random applications that have my location history, NSA and the othersnooping agencies can actually access spy on me easily? Wow! So my phone is actually a tracking device!"

Like Mr. Singh, people have no clue what is going on with their smartphones.

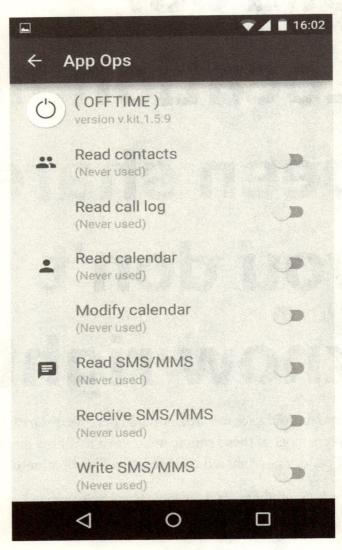

But now you can analyze your smartphones easily by installing an application called *Apps On*.

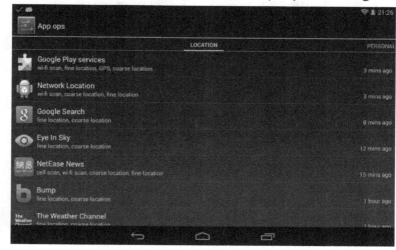

This application currently is only available for Android Phones.

You can review all applications and determine whether they allow sharing location, media etc. I strongly suggest everyone to be aware of his or her sharing services. Try installing only trusted applications, and do keep check whether you are being followed.

7. How to find lost iPhone?

Most important chapter, I feel. My Facebook inbox is just full of messages inquiring about this. I lost my cell phone please help me.

Steps to Find Lost iPhone:-

1. Always enable **Find my iPhone**, when you purchase a new device.

2. Go to *iCloud.com* and login with your apple username and password.

3. Now the next step is to put your device on lost mode. For this simply click on **Find My Phone**.

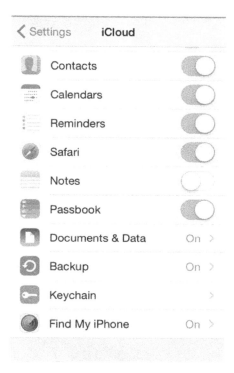

4. Now by activating **Lost mode** you can do following things:

- Lost Mode will automatically turn on the **location services** even it was disabled on your device.

- You can set up a **passcode**.

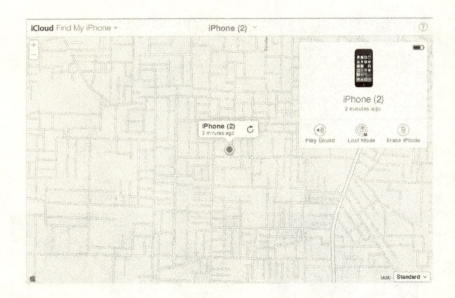

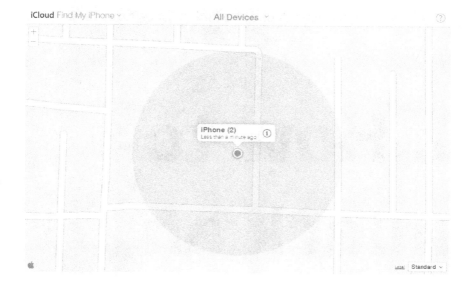

- You can also display a message on the **lock screen**.

- You can erase all data on your device remotely, just by clicking on **Erase** iPad, iPhone etc. But by doing so, you will not able to trace it further.

- If you did not enable **Find My iPhone** on your missing device in this case simply change your **iCloud password** so that no one can delete or make changes to your iCloud data.

- If you are unable to find your device by tracking then simply report your lost or stolen device to local law enforcement and your wireless carrier. Simply go to **supportprofile.apple.com** and know the serial number of all devices registered with your Apple ID.

8. How to unlock an iPhone passcode?

1. Go to icloud.com/find.

2. If prompted, sign in with your iCloud Apple ID.

3. Click All Devices at the top of your browser window.

4. Select the device you want to erase.

5. Click "Erase [device]" to erase your device and its passcode.

6. Use the Setup Assistant on your device to restore the most recent backup.

9. How to get fake likes on Instagram post?

Instagram has bestowed upon a lot of people with popularity and a fan base, predominantly by fake likes! I laughed hard when friend told me that her boy friend gets 5000+ Likes on his every photo at Instagram POST.

I asked her, "Is he Salman Khan"?

Anyone can get as many likes as they want.

How?

1. Install an Application called *Gain Likes*

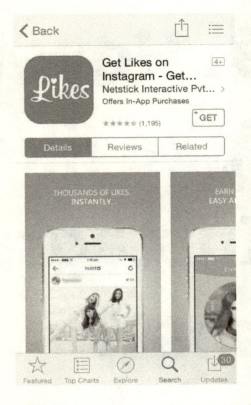

2. Buy Coins

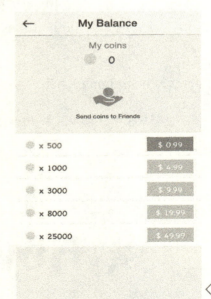

3. Choose photo, use coins and get likes.

10. How to get fake followers on Instagram?

Ever since I received my Punjabi Icon Award, I have been regularly visiting Mumbai. I observed that many youngsters have become popular just because they have more followers on Instagram. Girls start luring boys on their Instagram popularity!

Yes, I know this is very crazy, I got shocked too!!!

Then I analyzed 70% of these so called celebrities have fake followers. If you are teenager and belong to a metro city like Mumbai you can also become a celebrity within your group.

Here's how:

1. Install an Application called *Get Followers*.

2. Buy Coins

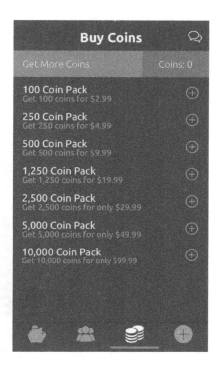

Enjoy the followers.

Cheers!

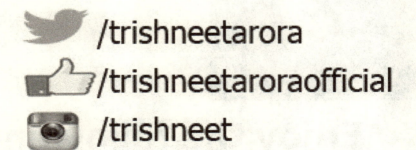

Printed in the USA
CPSIA information can be obtained
at www.ICGtesting.com
CBHW061202101224
18752CB00026B/125